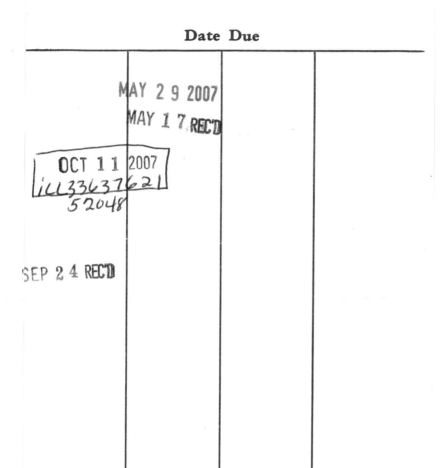

MADELEINE L'ENGLE

MADELEINE L'ENGLE

Author of
A Wrinkle in Time

A People in Focus Book

By Doreen Gonzales

dP **DILLON PRESS**
New York

Maxwell Macmillan Canada
Toronto

Maxwell Macmillan International
New York Oxford Singapore Sydney

To Chris, Todd, and Derek

Acknowledgments

A warm and special thank you to Madeleine L'Engle for the time and enthusiasm that she devoted to this project. Particular thanks to Larry Thompson at the Buswell Library in Wheaton, Illinois, to my editor, Shelley Sateren, and to Madeleine's assistant, Sheila Quinn. I am also grateful to the following people for their help with this book: Virginia C. Good, Edi King, Robert Lescher, David Maas, Margery N. Sly, and Thad A. Voss. Photographs have been provided by Beverly Hall, Madeleine L'Engle, David Maas, Smith College Archives, and Wheaton College Archives and Special Collections.

The following publishers have generously given permission to use extended quotations from copyrighted works: From A Wrinkle in Time, by Madeleine L'Engle. Copyright 1962 by Crosswicks, Ltd. Reprinted by permission of Farrar, Straus & Giroux, Inc. From And Both Were Young, by Madeleine L'Engle. Copyright 1983 by Crosswicks, Ltd. Reprinted by permission of Dell, a divison of the Bantam, Doubleday, Dell Publishing Group, Inc. From The Irrational Season, by Madeleine L'Engle. Copyright 1977 by Crosswicks, Ltd. Reprinted by permission of HarperCollins Publishers.

Library of Congress Cataloging-in-Publication Data

Gonzales, Doreen.
   Madeleine L'Engle : author of a wrinkle in time / by Doreen Gonzales.
     p. cm.— (A People in focus book)
   Includes bibliographical references and index.
   Summary: Describes the life and writing career of the novelist who won the Newbery Award for "A Wrinkle in Time."
   ISBN 0-87518-485-5
   1. L'Engle, Madeleine—Biography—Juvenile literature.
   2. Authors, American—20th century—Biography—Juvenile literature.
   [1. L'Engle, Madeleine. 2. Authors, American.] I. Title. II. Series.
PS3523.E55Z66 1991
813' .54—dc20   91-3883
[B]

Dillon Press
Macmillan Publishing Company
866 Third Avenue
New York, NY 10022

Maxwell Macmillan Canada, Inc.
1200 Eglinton Avenue East
Suite 200
Don Mills, Ontario M3C 3N1

Macmillan Publishing Company is part of the Maxwell Communication Group of Companies.

First edition
Printed in the United States of America
10   9   8   7   6   5   4   3   2

Contents

Chapter / One

Books, Operas, and Meals on a Tray

Meg's stomach seemed to drop, and she realized that the square box in which they stood must be an elevator and that they had started to move upward with great speed. The yellow light lit up their faces, and the pale blue of Charles's eyes absorbed the yellow and turned green.

Calvin licked his lips. "Where are we going?"

"Up." Charles continued his lecture. "On Camazotz we are all happy because we are all alike. Differences create problems. You know that, don't you, dear sister?"

"No," Meg said.

"Oh, yes, you do. You've seen at home how true it is. You know that's the reason you're not happy at school. Because you're different."

"Maybe I don't like being different," Meg said, "but I don't want to be like everybody else, either."

Are all of the people on the planet Camazotz truly happy? If you've read the classic children's science fiction story *A Wrinkle in Time*, then you know that the citizens of Camazotz are far from happy. The evil naked brain, It, has forced all of the people on Camazotz to walk, talk, think, and feel the same.

"Differences create problems," says six-year-old Charles, a visitor from earth. He has been hypnotized by It to believe that identical people are happy people.

Madeleine L'Engle, the author of *A Wrinkle in Time*, knows that differences sometimes create problems but that they can be blessings, too. In the early 1960s, she searched for two years to find a company to publish *A Wrinkle in Time*. During these years, more than thirty publishing houses rejected the story because it was too different from anything that had been published for children before.

After two years of rejections, Madeleine told her agent, "Send the manuscript back to me. Nobody's ever going to publish it, it's too peculiar...."

To Madeleine's surprise, a prestigious publishing company bought her "peculiar" story at last, and it went on to win the Newbery Medal in 1963. The Newbery

Madeleine as a baby in 1919.

Medal is the highest award the author of a children's book can receive. *A Wrinkle in Time* has been a runaway best-seller ever since.

Having a difference turn out to be a blessing in disguise was a new experience for Madeleine. During her childhood and teenage years, being different often made her unhappy. Like Meg Murry in *A Wrinkle in Time*, Madeleine spent her childhood feeling awkwardly different from her classmates and friends.

She was born on November 29, 1918, in New York City. Her father, Charles Wadsworth Camp, was overseas still in the aftermath of World War I on that snowy November day. He didn't see his daughter, little Madeleine L'Engle Camp, for the first time until six months later, when he came home from the war.

Before the war, Charles Wadsworth Camp worked as a newspaper reporter. He traveled all over the world on assignments, often taking his wife, Madeleine Barnett Camp, along. These exciting journeys ended after the war, but a new baby to care for was not the main reason. Madeleine's father's lungs had been damaged in the war by a poisonous chemical called mustard gas. Mustard gas goes on eating the lungs, making it easy for him to catch pneumonia, a frightening and often deadly disease in those days. Antibiotics hadn't yet been discovered.

Madeleine's father quit his job as a newspaper reporter soon after the war ended. He began writing short stories, movies, and plays, working in a small office in the famous Flatiron Building.

Madeleine's childhood home was a two-bedroom apartment on Eighty-second Street, near Central Park and the Metropolitan Museum of Art in New York City. Wealthy families lived on Park Avenue or Fifth Avenue. The Camps weren't rich, but they managed to live comfortably in this city and to enjoy its culture.

Baby Madeleine with her mother.

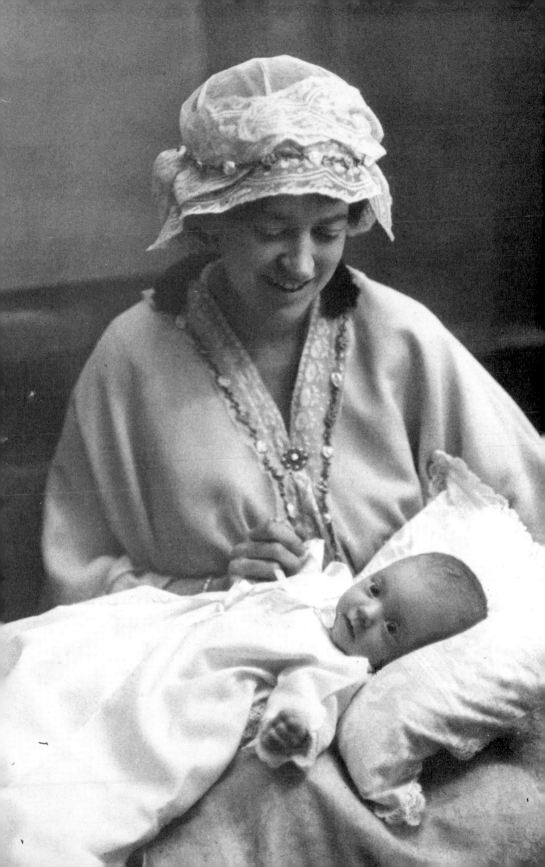

Madeleine's parents had very much wanted a baby, but once Madeleine arrived, they disagreed on how to raise her. Her father wanted a strict English upbringing for her, with dancing and piano lessons, a nanny, and meals on a tray in the nursery. Her mother didn't want this at all. She preferred that Madeleine be raised by a circus performer, who could teach her daughter to be confident and graceful.

This idea horrified Madeleine's father. He won the argument and hired Mrs. O'Connell, a nanny. Because of her father's wishes, Madeleine was raised very differently from most American children.

Mrs. O (as Madeleine called her) was a proper Englishwoman who, of course, never kissed young Madeleine good-night or held her hand. But she loved her, and broke rules by buying Madeleine packets of butterscotch in the park, for instance—and she was far from strict. Madeleine's mother wouldn't allow sugar on Madeleine's morning oatmeal, and she always tasted the bowl of hot cereal to make sure that no one had sweetened it. But Mrs. O secretly put sugar on the bottom of the bowl underneath the oatmeal, and stirred it in after Madeleine's mother had tasted the un-sweetened top layer. Madeleine's mother never understood why her little daughter ate oatmeal for Mrs. O and for nobody else!

Mrs. O made sure that Madeleine ate her morning

oatmeal. She also tried to change the fact that Madeleine was an overprotected child: She took the little girl on her first subway ride.

"She was probably the most normal part of my childhood," the grown-up Madeleine remembers about Mrs. O, "and I will always be grateful for her."

Madeleine enjoyed being a little spoiled by Mrs. O. Her parents were strict with her, and their busy lives kept them at a distance from their daughter. Madeleine's parents had been married for almost twenty years before Madeleine was born, and their interests were firmly planted in the world of art and politics, not in the world of paper dolls and made-up fairy tales.

Madeleine ate with her parents only at midday on Sundays. Years later, Mrs. Camp reminded her grown-up daughter about these Sunday meals: "We didn't know what to say to each other."

Looking back, the adult Madeleine admits this was true. She and her parents did not have many common interests to discuss over the dinner table. Madeleine preferred to eat alone in her room.

Madeleine's parents often hired household help besides Mrs. O. Her mother came from a world, now long gone, where there was almost always help in the kitchen. She was also quite frail and sometimes spent weeks in bed, with a white-uniformed nurse managing the household.

Madeleine's father was ill with his weak lungs much of the time, too. But in spite of her parents' illnesses, they went out to dinner many evenings, and then on to a play or concert. They always dressed elegantly. Madeleine's mother wore dresses in fashionable 1920s styles and her father often wore a top hat. The elegant couple kissed their daughter good-night before leaving for dinner.

With her parents either ill or away much of the time, Madeleine spent many days and evenings alone in her small bedroom. But she wasn't lonely. She happily ate her evening meals on a tray, her feet propped on her desk, a book in one hand and her fork in the other. After eating, she looked at more books or made up her own stories, illustrating them with pencil drawings or watercolor paintings.

Every day, her mother or Mrs. O read books out loud to Madeleine. By the time she was five, she knew every story in each of the books in her bookcase, many of them fairy tales.

Reading, inventing, and listening to stories were very important to this only child who spent many hours by herself. Madeleine wanted to be a writer at a very young age, from the time she was able to hold a pencil! She wrote her first story at age five, about a little "grul." "Grul" is how the young writer spelled "girl."

In 1924, six-year-old Madeleine began first grade at

Five-year-old Madeleine with Dearma, her grandmother, in Florida.

Madeleine on the sandy steps at Dearma's seaside cottage in Florida.

a private school in New York City. Oberlin was a small school for students in grades one, two, and three. By the end of her second year, Madeleine was able to read and write quite well. She was now able to read the more difficult books in her bookcase, without help from her mother, father, or Mrs. O.

That same year, Madeleine began piano lessons, which she loved. Her mother was an excellent pianist, and often played for friends who visited their apartment.

Many of these friends were actors, writers, musicians, and singers, and Madeleine's parents had a supper party for them every Sunday evening. Madeleine was supposed to be asleep before the guests arrived, but she usually stayed awake to hear the party sounds, which often centered around the piano. During the opera season, many of the guests were members of the Metropolitan Opera Company, and Mrs. Camp played opera scores while the singers sang along.

During many of these parties, Madeleine slipped out of her bedroom and quietly inched her way into the living room. She crawled behind the long, red sofa, ducked under the grand piano, and crouched behind the music rack to listen to the beautiful music. Her parents never discovered her hiding place, but at times the guests spied her. They seemed to find the music-loving youngster under the piano amusing, and didn't tell the unsuspecting parents.

When Madeleine turned eight, her father decided she was old enough to go to the opera, and he took her to a matinee of *Madama Butterfly*. Fascinated, Madeleine watched this classic opera about a teenage Japanese woman, Madame Butterfly, who marries a carefree American sailor. In the story, the sailor leaves Madame Butterfly to marry another woman, an American. Madame Butterfly is heartbroken over the loss of her love, and kills herself at the end of the opera.

This ending shocked the sensitive eight year old. She wasn't at all prepared for the opera to end so unhappily.

The next time her father took Madeleine to the opera, *I Pagliacci*, she asked, "Father, does this opera have an unhappy ending, too?"

Her father told his daughter that, yes, this opera also ended unhappily.

Madeleine began to cry. She sobbed and sobbed, until finally her father stood up and took her home. The curtains hadn't even opened for the first act.

That year, Madeleine began to keep a journal. She wrote frequently in her private journal, recording many details of things that she did, saw, and felt. This was the beginning of a lifelong habit for Madeleine.

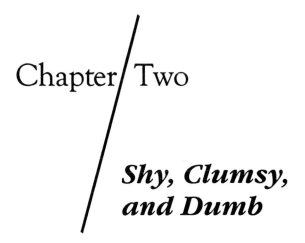

Chapter / Two

Shy, Clumsy, and Dumb

In the fourth grade, Madeleine had an attack of iritis, a painful swelling of the eye. Several months later, she had a second attack, and her doctor warned that a third attack would make her blind. For years after hearing this warning, Madeleine lived in fear of becoming blind. This made her very aware and appreciative of all the sights around her.

No one guessed how keenly Madeleine observed things, not even her mother. During family trips to Europe, her mother was certain that her young daughter saw nothing in their many tours of castles and museums. But years later, Madeleine amazed her mother by describing in detail people and places that she had seen during those childhood trips to Europe.

The adult Madeleine clearly remembers a childhood

On vacation with her parents in Europe, ten-year-old Madeleine poses
in a Breton costume for the camera.

summer evening in France, when she and her parents went to a tiny, one-ring circus. A shabby lion came out of its cage, paced in the small ring that was surrounded by a chicken wire fence, and roared. Terrified, Madeleine grabbed her parents' hands, expecting the lion to leap over the flimsy fence.

The young Madeleine observed closely all that she heard, smelled, tasted, and saw in Europe, such as this event at the tiny French circus. She stored the memories in her mind and in her journals, knowing that one day she would use many of them in her stories.

In 1928, Madeleine began fourth grade at another New York City private school with a fine reputation. Unfortunately for Madeleine, this school put great importance on athletics.

As a toddler, Madeleine had suffered an illness that left one of her legs shorter than the other, and when she was tired, she limped. So Madeleine was clumsy and a poor runner.

"Any team I was on lost automatically," the grown-up Madeleine recalls. She was always the last to be chosen, and her fourth-grade classmates groaned rudely when she joined their team.

Madeleine was very sensitive to the groans of her classmates. She couldn't shrug it off and pretend that it didn't matter. Her natural shyness grew worse, making her even more unpopular with her peers.

Madeleine's unpopularity at this school was not limited to the students. Her homeroom teacher believed that she was clumsy and dumb. This teacher began to show Madeleine's schoolwork to the class as examples of poor work. Sometimes, she held up Madeleine's papers and laughed at them in front of the class.

Before long, Madeleine stopped doing her schoolwork altogether. What was the point? she thought bitterly. Her teacher always found fault in her papers. Why bother?

Madeleine's lifelong image of herself formed at this school. For years to come, she would still think of herself as shy, clumsy, ugly, unpopular, and dumb.

Madeleine didn't tell her parents about her unhappiness at school. She knew she had to go to classes, whether she liked them or not. She could blame no one but herself, Madeleine believed, if things were unpleasant there.

Madeleine found comfort outside of school, in reading books and writing stories and poems. She read anything that she could find: fairy tales, old classics, the Bible. One of her very favorite books was *Emily of New Moon* by L. M. Montgomery. Emily, too, was determined to be a writer, and she, like Madeleine, knew how hard it was to write a good story. Madeleine reread *Emily of New Moon* many, many times—at least once a month for two years!

Madeleine's grandfather sent books to his grand-daughter each Christmas from London. Madeleine always sniffed her new books from England before reading them, because English printer's ink smelled differently than American ink. Madeleine enjoyed her books with four of her five senses—all except taste!

Madeleine loved getting books as gifts, because there wasn't a library near her family's Eighty-second Street apartment. After she had read her books count-less times, she often longed for new ones. When this happened, she knew that the only way to get new stories was to write them herself.

Most of the stories that Madeleine wrote during her elementary school years were make-believe. Writing fantasy stories helped soothe the pain of being an outcast at school. It also helped ease her growing fears at home on Eighty-second Street.

Madeleine's father's gas-burned lungs made him cough constantly, and the sound reminded Madeleine of war. "There won't be another war, will there?" Madeleine asked her parents, feeling deeply afraid of this possibility.

Her parents never lied to her. It was possible that there might be another world war soon, they admitted. Hearing this, Madeleine helped ease her fears of war by writing stories in which love was stronger than hate.

But Madeleine spent her childhood in the shadow

of an even greater fear: her father dying. Every day, his cough echoed through the small apartment. His lungs were getting worse, and he was slowly dying.

Dreaming exciting daydreams and writing stories with hopeful endings helped ease Madeleine's hurt feelings and her terrible fears. She wrote to keep herself company and she daydreamed—about glorious adventures in which she was graceful and fearless.

"My real life was not in school but in my stories and my dreams," the adult Madeleine recalls. "The people I lived with in books were far more real to me than my classmates. The Madeleine I wrote about in my stories was far more my real self than the self I took to school."

Ten-year-old Madeleine came home from school in the afternoons, set down her book bag, and thought to herself, I am the cripple, the unpopular one. Then she went to her room and wrote stories of make-believe. In every story, the heroine was always the kind of girl that Madeleine wanted to be.

Since Madeleine never took these stories to school, her teacher had no idea she wrote so much. The following spring, in 1930, when Madeleine was a sixth grader, she entered one of her poems in a school poetry contest and it won first prize. Her teacher was astonished when she heard that Madeleine was the winner.

"Madeleine isn't bright. She couldn't have written

that poem; she must have copied it," the teacher insisted.

Madeleine was dumbfounded. Her poem had won first prize, but now her teacher accused her of copying it!

Her homeroom teacher and classmates couldn't believe that Madeleine wrote poetry at all, much less good poetry. She never talked, she never smiled, she never did her homework. Her schoolwork was only good for laughing at. "Dumb" Madeleine Camp wrote a prizewinning poem? Never!

This contest had been for the entire school and was judged by the head of the English department for the upper school. Madeleine had given her poem directly to the judge, not to her teacher, as all of the students were supposed to do. If her teacher had seen it first, she surely wouldn't have allowed the "copied" poem to enter the competition.

Madeleine usually didn't tell her parents about her problems at school, but this time she couldn't hide her pain, bitterness, and tears. When she told her parents, her mother was angry and upset, too.

Right away, Madeleine's mother carried a stack of her daughter's stories and poems to the school to prove that the child loved to write. After much discussion, the school's authorities agreed that Madeleine could have written the winning poem after all.

Madeleine went home and wrote about the painful experience in her journal. She knew she would never forget how it stung to be falsely accused by a teacher!

Madeleine's parents didn't forget the bad experience, either. In the fall, they sent their daughter to Todhunter, a new private school in New York City.

Madeleine began sixth grade with a young, enthusiastic teacher who was on her first job. This teacher, Margaret Clapp, saw at once that Madeleine was a talented writer, and she encouraged her to write more.

Again, Madeleine's papers were held up to the class as examples. But this time they were shown as good examples, not bad ones.

One day that year, Madeleine came running into her apartment calling out to her mother, "Mother, Mother, you ought to scold me for the sin of gluttony!"

"Whatever for?" asked her mother.

"Miss Clapp liked my story so much that she read it out loud to the whole class, and I was so happy I just gloated and gloated!"

Miss Clapp saw that Madeleine had a fine mind. She pushed the twelve year old by assigning difficult books for her to read. The new ideas and words in these books challenged Madeleine to work harder than she had ever worked before. For the first time since she had left Oberlin, school was a joy. Miss Clapp was a truly great teacher who went on to be the first woman president of Wellesley College.

At home, Madeleine did her homework faithfully. When she finished her homework, she wrote stories and poems and played the piano.

Overshadowing Madeleine's happiness, however, was her father's poor health. During the winter of 1930-1931, Mr. Camp became ill with pneumonia. He went into the hospital, and both Madeleine and her mother worried that he might die.

After many long weeks, Mr. Camp grew well. But before he left the hospital, his doctor told him he must move away from New York City. His injured lungs were too weak for the city's dirty air. He needed to live where the air was clear and clean.

Madeleine felt torn. Of course she wanted her father to be healthy, but she didn't want to leave Todhunter School. Miss Clapp had made her feel valued and appreciated.

Years later, the adult Madeleine realized that during her sixth-grade year at Todhunter she had learned much more than reading, writing, and arithmetic from Miss Clapp. At Todhunter, her self-confidence had grown.

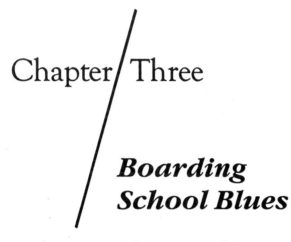

Chapter / Three

Boarding School Blues

In the spring of 1931, Madeleine and her parents moved away from New York City. They traveled to Europe with another family that had three boys. The two families rented a chateau in the French Alps near the village of Publier, France.

The chateau was inexpensive because it hadn't been altered since the eleventh century. Even before she unpacked, Madeleine was busy exploring its dozens of rooms. A huge fireplace filled one wall of the living room, and a small organ sat along another wall. Next to her parents' bedroom, Madeleine discovered a tiny, octagon-shaped chapel, complete with a kneeling board, called a *prie-dieu*, and stained glass windows.

The old house was charming, but the family missed the modern conveniences they were used to in

America. Each day, water had to be carried to the bedrooms for washing, and the only place to cook was over the fireplace.

The house also had no radio or phonograph, so beautiful music no longer filled their house. But the lack of music and modern conveniences was only a part of the parents' hardships in their new home. Madeleine's father grew weaker each day and felt pain every time he breathed. Her mother spent her days taking care of him as well as housekeeping and baby-sitting for the four children while the other parents went sight-seeing. She felt unhappily housebound and was also very worried about her husband's health. The stress in Madeleine's parents' daily lives drained them emotionally. They longed for the theater or the opera to take their minds off their troubles, but here in the remote region there was no entertainment at all.

Madeleine managed to stay happy by escaping into a world of make-believe. Every day she wandered through the house, dreaming up stories about the people who had lived there through the ages. Then she wrote and illustrated the stories in her notebooks.

One day that summer, the family drove down the mountain to Lake Geneva. Madeleine's parents let her take a kayak out onto the lake. Floating over the water, she gazed at the Alps rising around her, and she drifted into a deep daydream that lasted a long time.

Twelve-year-old Madeleine at Mount Blanc ski resort near Chamonix, France. The higher altitude at Chamonix helped Mr. Camp to breathe easier.

When she finally paddled the kayak back to the shore, her parents were furious. Why hadn't she come when they had called her? Her parents demanded an answer.

"I didn't hear anybody call," Madeleine protested.

But her mother didn't believe her. As punishment, Madeleine wasn't allowed to read or write for twenty-four hours. To Madeleine, this was the worst punishment possible, and she begged to be spanked instead. But her mother wouldn't give in.

At the end of that summer, Madeleine's father was still having trouble breathing, so the family moved higher into the Alps to Chamonix, also in France.

As they had done when she was younger, Madeleine's mother and father argued about what to do with her. Her mother wanted Madeleine to come with them and attend school in Chamonix. But her father didn't think that Madeleine would get a proper education there.

At last, her parents agreed to send Madeleine to a girls' boarding school on the other side of Lake Geneva. Chatelard School was near the town of Montreux, Switzerland.

When Madeleine's parents told her about Chatelard, she simply accepted their decision. She didn't know then how difficult this boarding school was going to be for her.

Years later, Madeleine wrote a book about this experience. Here is what Madeleine wrote in the book called *And Both Were Young*, about a girl named Flip who is being sent to boarding school:

> Something turned over in Flip's stomach. I should be ashamed, she thought. I should be ashamed to be so scared.
> But she was scared. She had never been separated, even for a night, from her entire family. Now she would be completely on her own. She remembered her mother shaking her once, and laughing at her, and saying, "Darling, darling, you must learn to be more independent, to stand on your own feet. You must *not* cling so to Father and me. Suppose something should happen to us? What would you do?" That thought was so preposterously horrible that Flip could not face it. She had flung her arms around her mother and hidden her head.

Twelve-year-old Madeleine clung to the hope that boarding school would be fun. But this hope evaporated the instant she arrived at Chatelard and met the woman in charge of the dormitory.

"If you have read boarding school stories, Madaleen, forget them," the matron told her sharply. "School is not like that."

Madeleine was the only American girl at Chatelard. She had also started school a week late, and by then all of the other girls had already made friends. They paid little attention to Madeleine, and she felt terribly lonely.

At the end of her first week at Chatelard, Madeleine realized she hadn't had a moment to herself the entire time, even without having any friends! There had been no time in the school's busy schedule for privacy or daydreaming. Madeleine knew that if she wanted to be a writer she had to have some quiet time alone with her imagination. She was determined to find that time for herself at Chatelard.

One evening, she took her pen and notebook and slipped into the bathroom to write a story. Surely, she thought, no one will bother me here. However, in only a few minutes a housemother pounded on the door.

"Who is in there?" she shouted. "What are you doing? Come out!"

There was no time for imagining during her classes, either. If she daydreamed in class, her teacher scolded her.

"What! Daydreaming again, Madeleine? You'll never get anywhere that way."

Without time for imagining, Madeleine felt cut off from a part of herself. She also thought that Chatelard's food was horrible, and she always felt cold in the poorly heated school buildings. After a short time at school that fall, she and other girls developed a skin condition called chilblains from the cold air in the buildings. Chilblains made their hands chap and bleed.

In her misery, Madeleine wrote to her parents, telling them that Chatelard was an awful place. In her letter she begged them to let her come home. Finally, a reply arrived from her parents. Their letter said that they had talked a long time about letting Madeleine come home. But they had decided that she should stay at Chatelard and learn from her experiences there.

Hot tears ran down Madeleine's cheeks. She read the letter over and over again, hardly believing her parents' reply.

Each night for three weeks, Madeleine stared out her window and cried until she fell asleep. Through her tears, she saw the spectacular white-capped Alps rising above Lake Geneva. The scene was like a storybook picture. It was a sight impossible to ignore, even in Madeleine's unhappiness, and before long she was making up stories about the mountains.

Little by little, Madeleine cried less at night and daydreamed more. After a while, bedtime became the most important part of her day—it was the time when she traveled far from her miseries at Chatelard and wrote stories in her mind.

Weeks passed, and Madeleine learned to make her days bearable, too. She learned to shut out the noises around her in order to dream and write anywhere she was—even in class when she was supposed to be listening to a lesson.

At first, the other girls at Chatelard thought Madeleine was odd. She didn't gossip. She showed no interest at all in joining the other girls in the recreation room after classes. Plus, she was always writing!

One morning, Madeleine sat at an all-school assembly watching a teacher take attendance at the front of the hall. As Madeleine waited for her name to be called, she sucked on a gold bridge that a dentist had made for her. The bridge fit onto the roof of Madeleine's mouth and had two false teeth attached to it, where two of Madeleine's teeth had never grown in.

Suddenly, the teacher calling roll saw that Madeleine had something in her mouth.

"Come here," the teacher barked, assuming that Madeleine had chewing gum in her mouth.

Madeleine walked up to the teacher while all of the girls in the school watched.

"Spit," the teacher commanded, holding out her hand.

Madeleine spat. What landed in the teacher's palm was not the gum she had expected, but Madeleine's wet bridge with the two small teeth attached to it. The horrified teacher stared at the bridge, too surprised to say a word.

This scene delighted Madeleine's classmates and from then on she was treated as one of them. "After that moment of glory I was allowed to be good at writing and bad at hockey and net ball," the adult Madeleine remembers.

At Christmastime that year, Madeleine returned to Chamonix for her vacation. For the first time, she saw how deeply unhappy her parents were. Madeleine's mother, who was not always well herself, continued to worry about her husband's health.

One afternoon, Madeleine went to her parents' bedroom to talk to her mother. She saw Mrs. Camp lying on the bed and was shocked by the expression of grief and despair on her mother's face. Never before had Madeleine realized how lonely and heartsick her mother felt. Quietly, Madeleine backed out of the room before her mother saw her.

During that Christmas vacation, the family went on a starlit sleigh ride. As the horses pulled them across the snow, Madeleine slipped into a world of make-believe—a world free from worry. But when the ride ended, she deliberately stopped her dreaming. She now knew that she could no longer hide from her parents' pain by escaping into her fantasies.

In the fall of 1932, Madeleine began eighth grade at Chatelard. All winter long, she and her roommates secretly read detective novels that they were not allowed to read. In one of the books, Madeleine read about opium, a drug that comes from the poppy plant and gives people beautiful dreams.

Madeleine was curious about opium visions. Could she have these visions, too? she wondered. In the spring, when all of the girls at Chatelard planted small gardens, she and a classmate planted poppy seeds.

When their plants blossomed, the girls ate poppy flower sandwiches, poppy leaf sandwiches, and poppy seed sandwiches. Because they were allowed no time for daytime dreaming, they had to dream at night. They soon learned that they did not need poppy sandwiches in order to have exciting dreams.

Later that spring, Madeleine received a letter from her parents. It was about Dearma, Madeleine's grandmother who lived in Florida. The letter said that Dearma was seriously ill, and that the family would have to move back to America to live with her when Madeleine's school term was over.

Madeleine was fourteen years old when she and her parents moved to the beach house that they called Illyria. Each morning at Illyria, Madeleine swam in the ocean, then sat on the beach to read or daydream. Sometimes she wrote stories or poems.

When her father was well enough, he and Madeleine took long walks along the sand, and she read her poems to him. Sometimes he just listened and

Fourteen-year-old Madeleine at Illyria, holding her dog Sputstzi.

nodded his head. But when her father said, "Now there's a poem," Madeleine knew she had written something special. She wrote this poem during her time at Illyria:

Wind Fancy
The wind blows on the golden sand
And forms a dusty fairyland.
The gauzy swirls are elfin things
That flutter by on wispy wings,
And bubbles from the foam-flecked waves
Are jewels from the fairy caves.

That fall, her parents sent her to Ashley Hall Boarding School in Charleston, South Carolina, where she began ninth grade. At Ashley Hall, Madeleine blossomed and experienced something new—being popular with her peers.

"I loved Ashley Hall, where for the first time I was happy in school," recalls the adult Madeleine. "At Ashley Hall I found my stride and was appreciated and a leader."

Madeleine joined clubs and participated in school plays at Ashley Hall. In 1934 and 1935, she was elected to Ashley Hall's student council. During her senior year, 1936–1937, Madeleine was the student council president.

But in the flurry of all her activities, Madeleine's real love, writing, was not forgotten. During her four years at Ashley Hall, she wrote scores of stories and poems. In 1936, one of her poems won the school poetry prize. Much of Madeleine's writing was published in Ashley Hall's literary magazine. In her last year, she was chosen to be the editor of the magazine.

Though Madeleine began her senior year full of confidence and joy, one autumn day she received a letter from home that brought her stable world crashing down.

Her mother had written, "Father is in the hospital with pneumonia. Please write to him. Pray for him, and for me, too."

Madeleine immediately mailed her father three poems that she had written, intuitively knowing that they would not reach her father in time.

The next day, the principal called Madeleine to her office. She told her she was to take the evening train home. On the train, Madeleine tried to read a book called *Jane Eyre*, but she couldn't concentrate. Instead, she prayed. "Please, God, do whatever is best. For Father, for Mother. Please do whatever is best."

Chapter / Four

No More Made–Up Fairy Tales

By the time Madeleine reached Florida, her father had died. When she heard the news, she felt numb and empty and couldn't cry.

Madeleine didn't cry at her father's funeral. She pushed her grief deep inside her, trying to be brave. On the outside, she appeared calm to her mother and other relatives. But on the inside, she felt great pain and was asking herself many troubling questions about death: What had happened to her father? Where was he? Had he just stopped existing? Even someone brought up to believe in God asks these questions.

A few days after the funeral, Madeleine returned to Ashley Hall. As soon as she could, she climbed into an old oak tree with her journal and wrote, "Father died." That was all. She buried her feelings and ignored the huge hole in her life her father's dying had created. In the spring, Madeleine tried to write a story about her father's death, but she knew she didn't get the story right, and she put it away.

Madeleine's busy days at high school helped her to avoid her feelings. It was now her senior year and she was immersed in a whirlwind of schoolwork and extracurricular activities. She was also busy considering what she would do when she graduated in May.

The principal at Ashley Hall, Mary Vardine McBee, wanted Madeleine to go on to college at Smith, an all-girl Ivy League school in Massachusetts. Smith College was small and prestigious. Madeleine's grandfather had set up a trust fund for his grandchildren's college education, so Smith was in the realm of possibility. A girl had to have an excellent high school record as well as high scores on college entrance tests to be accepted there. Even though Madeleine didn't think she would pass the college entrance tests, she signed up to take them because Miss McBee wanted her to.

In June of 1937, Madeleine graduated from Ashley Hall. Right away, she enrolled in a summer class that would help her review for the college entrance tests. Madeleine met a girl named Pat in this review class. Pat was tall and awkward, and she reminded Madeleine of herself. The two girls became friends immediately, and their friendship was to last a lifetime.

Madeleine took her college entrance tests at the end of the class. Then she and her mother went to Europe for the remainder of the summer. Madeleine decided that if she didn't pass the tests, she would stay in Europe and write a novel.

Meanwhile, the professors at Smith College looked over Madeleine's tests. Her mathematics scores were low, but her long, handwritten answers on the English examinations were the best they had ever seen. On this strength, she was accepted into Smith. Madeleine received Smith's letter of acceptance in Europe, and she was amazed that she passed the tests. She and her mother returned at once to Illyria and quickly packed Madeleine's bags and trunks for college.

Eighteen-year-old Madeleine said good-bye to her mother and traveled alone from Florida to Massachusetts by train. Shortly after Madeleine left for college, her mother was forced to sell Illyria for financial reasons, and she moved to an apartment in Jacksonville, Florida. When Madeleine heard this, she grieved for the oceanside cottage, which she had loved. But she was soon swept into the activities of her freshman year and there was no more time for grieving.

Madeleine majored in English. In her English classes, she studied great writers and took time to compose her own stories and poems. When she learned that Smith didn't have a literary magazine, she and a

classmate set out to create one. During her four years at Smith, Madeleine wrote dozens of poems and short stories, many of which were published in this new literary magazine. One of Madeleine's poems won the college's Elizabeth Babcock Poetry Prize, and she received $2,500 in prize money.

Madeleine had to take other classes at Smith besides English, though she considered them a waste of time. Occasionally, she skipped classes. But even so, her grades were always good. "College," Madeleine recalled years later, "is where I learned to work hard," in a way that benefited her throughout her life.

When she wasn't working hard at her schoolwork, Madeleine was busy with extracurricular activities. She wrote plays, and a few of them were performed by Smith students for the public. Madeleine acted in several Smith plays, too. She loved the theater and thought it was a wonderful place for a writer to learn about life and human nature.

Between attending classes, writing, and acting, Madeleine squeezed in visits to her friend Pat, who was at Vassar, fifty miles away. Madeleine also visited her mother in Florida each holiday. When family friends knew Madeleine would be home for a holiday, they invited her to fancy dances that they gave for their daughters.

Madeleine hated these dances. She was tall and

Paradise Pond at Smith College. Madeleine wrote some of her fiction and poetry on the banks of this pond during her college years.

Madeleine (on the right) *as the old nurse in Chekhov's* The Three Sisters, *performed by Smith students for the public.*

The Smith College Dramatic Association. Madeleine is seated on the couch (far left).

clumsy, and she felt like an ugly duckling who would never grow beautiful. She was ashamed to wear her glasses at these parties that bustled with attractive young people, so she didn't wear them even though she could barely see! Madeleine felt completely out of place and she was a stranger among these young people who had always known one another. Madeleine had to struggle to make conversation with her dates.

At one party, Madeleine's cousin helped her by writing a list of friendly questions that she could ask boys with whom she danced. Again, Madeleine did not wear her glasses and her dance partners' faces were a blur. Through the evening, she repeated her memorized friendly questions to her various dance partners. Just when she thought the evening was going well, a boy she was dancing with blurted out, "Hey, honey, what's your line? You've already asked me these same questions three times before."

Madeleine was too embarrassed to admit she hadn't recognized the boy without her glasses. "Well, you really haven't answered them properly," she replied.

"You really want to know?" the boy asked.

"Of course, or I wouldn't have kept asking."

Embarrassing incidents such as these made Madeleine invent all sorts of reasons to escape to the bathroom. Sometimes she purposely ripped the hem on her dress just so she could hide from the party for a while.

Although Madeleine never told her mother how much she despised these dances, their friendship deepened after her father's death. During vacations, mother and daughter traveled together and visited theaters, museums, operas, and restaurants. When Madeleine had to return to school and they couldn't be together, she wrote her mother a postcard every day.

As they grew closer, Madeleine sometimes shared her stories with her mother. In many ways, her father's death changed Madeleine's writing style and the subjects of her fiction. Now she wrote about real life and not made-up fairy tales. Though she didn't realize it yet, these new stories were about her own life. Many were about a man and woman who lived in Europe with their daughter. Madeleine clearly described the flaws and weaknesses of the parents in these stories. Madeleine's mother knew that there was no intention to hurt. She also recognized Madeleine's talent and always urged her to continue writing. She would tell Madeleine, "But it's a good story. It's very good. Keep on."

By the time Madeleine had begun her second year at college, she still hadn't allowed herself to mourn her father's death. These buried emotions led to a deep depression in the middle of her sophomore year. She was able to perform normally on the outside, but on the inside she was greatly troubled. Writing helped. Gradually, she began to recognize her own experiences and feelings in her stories. Finally, two years after her father's death, Madeleine broke down and cried. Slowly her depression went away.

In June of 1941, Madeleine graduated from Smith with honors. She dreamed of becoming a professional writer, but she also knew it would be several years before she could earn a living by writing alone. In the meantime, Madeleine decided she would act.

That fall, she moved back to New York City, and with three college friends rented an apartment on

Madeleine's graduation photograph, printed in Smith College's 1941 yearbook.

Ninth Street (a few miles from her childhood home). As soon as she was settled, Madeleine began to look for an acting job. She auditioned for a play called *Uncle Harry* and got a small part as well as the understudy position.

As understudy, Madeleine memorized the lines of the other actresses. Then, if one of them was sick and couldn't perform, Madeleine could quickly take over the part. For these two jobs, Madeleine was paid sixty-five dollars a week. But better than that, she was on Broadway!

Between rehearsals and shows, Madeleine tried to write. But the noise and activities of her three roommates were distracting. In the summer of 1942, she moved into a small apartment in Greenwich Village to live by herself. Now she could spend her days reading and writing as much as she wanted, without distractions. During this time that she lived in Greenwich Village, several of her stories were published in small magazines.

Knowing she needed to earn more money to make ends meet, Madeleine began sending her stories to national magazines. She decided to use only her first and middle names—Madeleine L'Engle—when she sent her stories to publishing companies. When her mother learned about this, she was hurt, thinking that Madeleine was rejecting her father by not keeping his last name. But Madeleine explained to her mother that because her father had been a writer and many publishers knew him, she didn't want her work to be accepted because of her father's old friendships with these publishers. She wanted to be considered a writer on her own merit, apart from her father's success in the publishing world.

Her first summer in Greenwich Village, Madeleine worked to finish a novel she had begun in college. The book, called *The Small Rain*, was about a concert

pianist. By that fall, Madeleine had finished the novel and she went back to acting, going on tour with the show *Uncle Harry.*

In the spring of 1943, she took *The Small Rain* to Vanguard Press, a book publishing company in New York City. An editor there, Bernard Perry, liked the book, though he thought parts of it needed to be rewritten. Madeleine went straight to work and spent her summer days making the changes. Each morning she went right to her typewriter, sometimes forgetting to eat breakfast.

At last, Madeleine finished the rewrite and took *The Small Rain* back to Vanguard. The editors liked her changes and bought the book. Madeleine was overjoyed!

Yet it would be a while before her book would earn any money, so she continued acting. Madeleine auditioned for a production of *The Cherry Orchard,* and again got a small part and the understudy position.

In 1944, a publishing company called Baker Books decided to publish a play Madeleine had written in college, called *18 Washington Square, South.* Also that year, *Mademoiselle* magazine bought one of her stories for two hundred dollars. Madeleine used this money to rent a slightly bigger apartment. Her small Greenwich Village apartment had no real kitchen, and Madeleine liked to cook and have guests for dinner. But cooking was nearly impossible with her tiny

Madeleine in 1942, when she lived in Greenwich Village.

refrigerator, two-burner stove, and no sink; dishes were washed in the bathtub. However, after selling the story to *Mademoiselle*, she found an apartment with a full-size kitchen on Tenth Street for five dollars more a month.

That summer, a few new actors were hired for some of the parts in *The Cherry Orchard*. An actor named Hugh Franklin was hired for an important male role. Madeleine had never heard of him, but her friends had seen him in other plays.

Madeleine watched Hugh during the first rehearsal. She could see that he was a fine actor. She also saw that he was tall and handsome, with dark hair and big blue eyes. Madeleine was sure that Hugh would never notice her, an actress with only a bit part as a clumsy maid.

But Hugh did notice Madeleine. At the end of the first rehearsal, he asked her to have lunch with him at a nearby diner. Madeleine and Hugh ate hamburgers, then continued to sit at the diner and talk—for nearly ten hours! It was two o'clock in the morning when Madeleine finally got home. As she let herself into her apartment, she thought, I have met the man I want to marry.

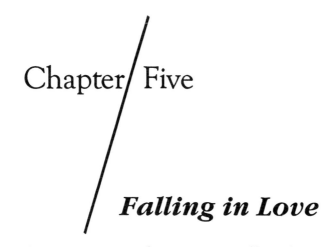

Chapter/Five

Falling in Love

On an autumn day in 1944, all of the actors in *The Cherry Orchard* climbed aboard a train in New York City. Their cross-country tour had begun.

On the first day of the tour, Hugh Franklin sat beside Madeleine on the train. Every time the train stopped in a new city, Hugh sat back down beside Madeleine after each stop. Everyone in the acting company could see that something romantic and special was happening between Madeleine and Hugh.

In Madison, Wisconsin, the two went for a long walk, holding hands and kicking fallen leaves. On another day, they took a riverboat ride in St. Louis, and later, in Chicago, they went to see plays alone together.

Madeleine knew she was falling in love with Hugh. But did Hugh love her? She wasn't sure and she didn't dare ask him. Somehow Madeleine felt sure of only one thing: If she pushed herself on Hugh, he would pull away.

One day in December, Hugh boarded the train and didn't sit next to Madeleine. She was stunned. They hadn't had an argument, so she wondered what on earth was wrong. Everyone in the company noticed the change in Hugh's behavior and wondered what had happened. He was acting so cold toward Madeleine! Her heart ached, but she tried to hide her feelings and pretend nothing was wrong.

By Christmas, Hugh was still avoiding Madeleine. She was relieved when the tour finally ended the following spring. Ever since Hugh had stopped dating her, she had been miserable, but she was determined not to chase after him.

Madeleine returned to her New York City apartment, and spent the spring days writing, reading, and playing her piano. She dated a few other men and had old friends over to dinner. But her world seemed empty without Hugh.

That April, Madeleine heard the news that President Roosevelt had died. She was upset and immediately thought of Hugh, who had admired the president a great deal. She called Hugh to say how sorry she was, and he sounded happy to hear from her. But as Madeleine hung up, she vowed never to call him again.

Many weeks went by as Madeleine kept her promise.

Early that summer, Hugh telephoned Madeleine and invited her to dinner. As they ate, he told her many personal and private things about his childhood. Later that evening, Madeleine thought a long time about this conversation and made a decision about it. A man does not talk that openly and vulnerably to a woman he does not intend to marry, she thought.

Hugh was away from New York all summer acting. In the fall, he went on tour with a play called *The Joyous Season*. While he was gone, Madeleine didn't receive any word from him, not even a postcard. She continued to date other men, and she spent her days working on her second novel, *Ilsa*. She kept busy, but Hugh was on her mind often. She couldn't stop thinking about the conversation they had in the summer.

When *The Joyous Season* returned to New York in early December, Hugh called and invited Madeleine to dinner. After eating a fine meal at a restaurant, they went to her apartment to talk. Hugh put "Swan Lake" on the phonograph, the waltz that had been played in each performance of *The Cherry Orchard*. The music reminded Madeleine of the early weeks of the tour, when she and Hugh had been so happy together. As the music played, Hugh pulled a book of Conrad Aiken's poetry off the bookshelf. He opened the book and began to read:

Music I heard with you was more than music,
And bread I broke with you was more than bread.

Then he turned to Madeleine and asked,
"Madeleine, will you marry me?"

"Yes," she replied, filled with joy.

The two sat down at once and excitedly talked
about their plans for the future. Madeleine told Hugh
that she wanted children of course, but that she wasn't
about to stop writing to be a perfect housewife! Hugh
agreed that he wanted a family, even though his acting
would often take him away from home. He also wanted
Madeleine to understand that he might not always earn
a steady income.

The two talked late into the evening. When Hugh
left it was long after midnight, but Madeleine was so
excited she couldn't sleep. Instead, she took a favorite
collection of Hans Christian Andersen stories off the
shelf and read the fairy tales until dawn.

Madeleine called her mother in the morning, but
was met with a lack of enthusiasm about the news.
Madeleine's mother didn't know Hugh and wasn't
sure an actor could support a family. But she could
certainly tell that her daughter was in love!

In January of 1946, *The Joyous Season* went on tour
and Madeleine was hired for the female understudy
position. During the tour, she continued to write

Hugh and Madeleine, shortly after their marriage in 1946.

fiction whenever she could—late in the evenings and early in the mornings. She even wrote backstage during performances, using her old boarding school trick of blocking out noises.

When the tour reached Chicago, Madeleine and Hugh decided that they couldn't wait another minute to get married! They searched for a church and at eleven o'clock in the morning on January 26, they were married at St. Chrysostom's Episcopal Church. Besides themselves and the priest, only two other people observed the service: two friends who acted as witnesses.

Immediately after the ceremony, Madeleine and Hugh hurried back to the theater to give two performances of *The Joyous Season*. After the final show that evening, they spent their wedding night in the luxurious bridal suite at the famous Edgewater Beach Hotel. The next day they moved to a much less expensive hotel.

When *The Joyous Season* closed in the spring, Madeleine and Hugh bought an old car and drove to Tulsa, Oklahoma, where Hugh's family lived. Next, they traveled to Jacksonville, Florida, so that Hugh could meet Madeleine's relatives. After their visit, they returned to New York, and Hugh moved into Madeleine's apartment on Tenth Street.

One spring weekend, Madeleine and Hugh went to visit some friends of Hugh's who lived in northwest Connecticut and who wanted to meet the bride. They showed the young couple a two-hundred-year-old farmhouse that was for sale. It sat on the crest of a hill, near the town of Goshen. Inside the white clapboard house, the wide-board floors were crooked and ancient wallpaper hung in strips from the walls. A room in the house had been used as a chicken coop and it was still full of hay and manure! Outside, a rickety porch clung to the front of the structure.

The farmhouse was in bad shape, but from the moment they saw it, Madeleine and Hugh were charmed

Crosswicks.

by it. The house itself was actually sturdy and solid. What it needed was cleaning and minor repairs. There were woods and pastures nearby, and a brook with a stone bridge that would make a perfect "thinking spot" for Madeleine. Before the weekend was over, they had bought the house.

Madeleine and Hugh spent the next few months fixing up their new home. They continued to live in New York but made frequent trips to Connecticut to work on the farmhouse. They sanded floors, painted walls, scrubbed everything, and tore down the old porch. They cleaned out the chicken-coop room and made it into a study for Madeleine.

That summer, Hugh was driving home from a summer theater job when a bee flew in the car window. The pesky bee buzzed around Hugh's face and he slowed down to twenty miles per hour while he tried to shoo the bee back out the window.

Just then, the car's right front tire blew out. Because Hugh was only driving twenty miles per hour, he was able to pull the car safely to the side of the road. Had he been driving faster, the tire blowout would have caused an accident that could have killed him.

This incident scared Madeleine and reminded her of how unpredictable life can be. Though she had previously wanted to wait two years before beginning a family, she agreed with Hugh it was time to start now.

The following June, Madeleine and Hugh had a baby girl. They named her Josephine. One night in late July, Madeleine became very ill because of complications from Josephine's birth. She had to have an operation and then spend a month in the hospital recovering.

When Madeleine came home at last and grew stronger, she concentrated on developing a routine that would allow her to be both a writer and a mother. She began to put Josephine to bed when Hugh left for the

Madeleine holding Josephine.

Josephine and her mother on an afternoon outing.

theater in the evenings. Then she wrote. When Hugh came home at midnight, they woke up Josephine and played with her until 2:00 A.M. Then they all went to bed. Hugh and Madeleine knew this schedule was peculiar, but it gave Madeleine time to write.

Her second novel, *Ilsa*, had now been published, and she was working on a third. But this novel wasn't going well, and Madeleine put it aside.

The next summer, Madeleine and Hugh moved to their country house in Connecticut, which they named Crosswicks. Hugh was gone much of the summer acting in various shows. While he was away, Madeleine began a new novel called *And Both Were Young*. She had been worried about her writing ability since her third novel hadn't gone well, but this book turned out nicely and was accepted for publication.

In the fall, Madeleine and Hugh moved back to an apartment in New York. During the next three years, they spent their summers at Crosswicks and their winters in New York City.

Madeleine wrote *Camilla* in 1949. She tried and tried to sell this novel, and was heartsick when no one bought it. Madeleine wrote about her disappointment in her journal. "The kitchen looks superb and glamourous," she recorded in her journal the day a new kitchen floor was installed at Crosswicks. "But because of poor rejected *Camilla*, it has lost half its glory."

Hugh pushes Josephine on a swing in a New York City park. Hugh,
Josephine, and Madeleine lived in the city in the wintertime.

Finally, to Madeleine's great relief, a publishing company called Simon and Schuster accepted *Camilla*.

Hugh's acting kept him away from home much of the time. One year, Madeleine and Hugh were together for only two weeks! During these times when he was away, Madeleine knew that pretty young actresses sometimes flirted with him. But she also knew that Hugh took his marriage vows seriously and would be faithful.

Each time a play ended, Hugh, like most actors, feared he wouldn't get another acting job. But he always did, and he got good parts, too. Frequently, he acted on television. Then Madeleine would sit with Josephine at a neighborhood bar, sipping ginger ale and watching Hugh on the television set in the bar, since they didn't have one of their own.

Madeleine and Hugh wanted a larger family, but because Hugh was away so much and neither one of them had a stable job, having another baby didn't seem wise. Madeleine and Hugh began to consider moving to Crosswicks to live there year-round. Then Hugh would get a job in the nearby town of Torrington, and they could raise a bigger family in the country as two full-time parents.

When Madeleine became pregnant in the summer of 1951, she and Hugh decided the time had come to live at Crosswicks full-time. Hugh went on one last acting tour and returned in the fall to look for a job in Connecticut near Crosswicks.

By March of 1952, Hugh still had not found a job. But Madeleine and Hugh were glad of this when their son Bion was born on March 24. Bion's birth was even harder for Madeleine than Josephine's birth. Hugh was needed at home to help take care of the children as Madeleine recovered.

Soon after Bion's birth, the general store in Goshen was put up for sale. It was run-down and had little business. The owner didn't have time to fix up the store, but he didn't want to see it closed down, either. He suggested that the Franklins buy it.

At first it seemed like a crazy idea. Neither Hugh nor Madeleine had any experience in business. But on the other hand, they thought, the store could provide them with a steady income if it was built into a good business. Hugh accepted the challenge and set right to work.

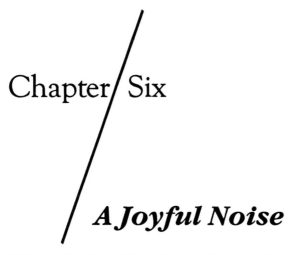

Chapter / Six

A Joyful Noise

When the Franklins first took over the store, business was slow, and they didn't make much money. But gradually, business improved. The town's tiny post office was in the store, and when people came in to pick up their mail, they often bought some of the basic groceries that Hugh stocked. About half of the customers were farmers, and Hugh stocked things they needed, too. Two of his best-selling items were products for dairy cows. Within a year, the store was doing well, and the Franklins were earning a modest but steady income.

Madeleine worked in the store for a few hours each day. This forced her to overcome her natural shyness. "One cannot be shy behind the counter," says Madeleine.

Many of the Franklins' customers became lifelong

friends. Madeleine and Hugh also made friends at the Goshen church where they taught Sunday school and Madeleine directed the choir. These friends helped one another whenever they were needed. Hugh regularly drove the tractor for his neighbor during harvesting season, and each year the women helped each other can and freeze the vegetables from their gardens.

Madeleine was grateful for this helpful community because living at Crosswicks was harder than she had expected. She washed laundry in a machine that froze once a week and cooked in a drafty kitchen that was rarely warmer than fifty-five degrees. When her children wanted playmates, she had to drive the playmates back and forth, since the Franklins lived in the country and it was too far for the children to walk.

Unfortunately, all of her family responsibilities left Madeleine with little free time to write. Sometimes she grumbled about how her life was different from the authors she admired. "Emily Brontë didn't have to run the vacuum cleaner," she grumbled. "Jane Austen didn't do the cooking."

During a particularly frustrating week, it seemed that the Franklin children couldn't eat a meal without somebody spilling milk. One night, Madeleine announced, "Whoever spills the next glass of milk will leave the room!" Seconds later, Madeleine knocked over her glass. Without a word, she left the room.

Though it wasn't easy, Madeleine managed to write some fiction and poetry while her children were growing up. She read, too, as many as three full-length adult books a week. She even read while cooking and taking baths! She also managed to squeeze in one hour of quiet conversation with Hugh every day. In addition, most days Madeleine took time to write in her journal.

Madeleine was not only busy with her home, husband, children, and their playmates, but also with pets and frequent house guests. Each year, Madeleine's mother stayed at Crosswicks for a month, and once, a baby-sitter who came for an evening stayed for two years! Homeless animals were always welcome at Crosswicks, too, and often several cats, dogs, and birds lived there at the same time.

"There's an odd law about families," says Madeleine, "they tend to grow; it may be dogs, or cats, or babies, or birds, or plants, but families need to blossom. Our family grew in all kinds of ways, for Hugh taught me early that a family with closed doors is not a family."

In 1956, the Franklin family grew again. Early on a November morning, Madeleine and Hugh learned that Liz, one of Madeleine's closest friends, had died. Liz's husband had died a year earlier, so now their seven-year-old daughter, Maria, was without parents. Madeleine and Hugh opened their arms to Maria and

Madeleine and Bion in 1954.

brought her to Crosswicks to live with them, officially adopting her in 1957.

The three Franklin children filled the days at Crosswicks with what Madeleine called "a joyful noise." Bedtime was more peaceful, as Madeleine read and sang to the children and listened to their prayers. After tucking her children in, she went to her typewriter and worked late into the nights, often falling asleep at her desk. In the mornings, Hugh made breakfast and took the children to school so Madeleine could sleep late.

When Bion, the youngest child, began school, Madeleine at last had more time to write. She began a novel called *Meet the Austins.* "[The book] came directly out of our lives at that time," recalls Madeleine. "It could easily have been called *Meet the Franklins!*"

Meet the Austins wasn't published until 1960. During the 1950s, almost no one wanted to buy Madeleine's work. Between 1952 and 1959, she sent out hundreds of pages of writing but sold only a few poems, two short stories, and one book called *A Winter's Love.*

The numerous rejections hurt Madeleine deeply. Whenever a manuscript was turned down, she walked along the dirt road by Crosswicks and cried. Madeleine's agent feared all of these disappointments would make her stop writing. But Madeleine wouldn't give up. With each rejection, she allowed herself twenty-four

The Franklin children in the church choir: Bion, age 5 (front row, second from the right); Maria, age 9 (second row, fourth from the left); Josephine, age 11 (behind Maria).

hours of private unhappiness—then she turned back to life.

In the fall of 1958, Madeleine looked forward to turning forty. During her thirties, her roles as mother, writer, housekeeper, storekeeper, and choir director had been exhausting. She was also very weary after a full decade of receiving rejection slips! Surely, she thought, my forties will bring me better luck as a writer.

On the day of her fortieth birthday, Madeleine was in her study writing. When the phone rang, her heart leaped. Maybe it was the publisher who was reading her book, *The Lost Innocent!*

It wasn't. It was Hugh calling from the store to say

he had received a letter for her. "I'm sorry to have to tell you this on your birthday," he said, "but you'd never trust me again if I kept it from you. [The publisher] has rejected *The Lost Innocent*."

Tears poured from Madeleine's eyes. She walked around and around her study, sobbing. She thought about all the hours she had spent writing instead of doing other things. She could have been a better housewife—scrubbing her floors or learning to make pie crusts. Or she could have been earning more money doing something else, working at a paying job to help the family's income.

As Madeleine sobbed, she made a decision: She would stop wasting her time writing and become a better wife and mother! She covered up her typewriter.

A moment later, she was struck with an idea for another book and the story began to take shape in her mind. Suddenly, Madeleine smiled. She couldn't give up writing, she realized, even if she never sold another book! Writing was a part of what made her Madeleine. She wiped away her tears, uncovered her typewriter, and went back to work.

More and more, Madeleine missed being in New York City, where plays, art exhibits, and other writers sparked ideas in her mind. Hugh, too, was lonely for the city. He longed to act again. One night, Madeleine asked him, "Are you really still happy with the store?"

"No, not now," he answered.

"Then sell it," Madeleine suggested, and they agreed it was time to return to New York City. They would keep Crosswicks as a summer home.

Knowing the move would be hardest for the children, Hugh explained to them how New York would be different from Goshen. For instance, he told them, their seven cats and three dogs could not live in the city.

"We will take one cat and one dog," he said.

With wide eyes, Bion asked, "And one child, Daddy?"

In 1959, the Franklins sold their store. In early May they left Crosswicks to go on a ten-week camping trip across the United States. Every day, Madeleine wrote in her journal about what she experienced during the journey. Somewhere in New Mexico, three names popped into her head—Mrs Who, Mrs Whatsit, and Mrs Which. She had no idea what made her think of these names or what she would do with them. But she wrote them down in her journal, believing that one day she would discover their purpose.

In Helena, Montana, Hugh received a letter offering him a role in a Broadway play. Knowing this was his chance to get back into the theater, the Franklins hurried to New York City. Hugh rented a hotel room and began rehearsals. Madeleine and the children returned to Crosswicks for the time being, until the family could find an apartment in the city.

Back at Crosswicks, Madeleine continued to read Albert Einstein's theories about time and time travel and Planck's quantum theory. Their ideas fascinated her, and soon her imagination was creating a science fiction story.

She wrote her story quickly, in what she calls a "white heat." The book included three supernatural creatures who traveled through time. When she needed names for these creatures, Madeleine knew just what to call them—Mrs Who, Mrs Whatsit, and Mrs Which! She finished her book in the fall of 1959 and named it A Wrinkle in Time.

"[A Wrinkle in Time] was very different from my six earlier published books but I loved it," Madeleine recalls, "and I hoped that it would mark a turning point."

But one publisher after another turned it down. Some thought the story talked about evil too much; others felt it was too difficult for children to understand.

These rejections made Madeleine very unhappy. One night, she marched down the lane at Crosswicks and yelled up at God, "Why don't you let it get accepted? Why are you letting me have all these rejection slips? You know it's a good book! I wrote it for you!"

That January, Madeleine finally found a suitable apartment in New York City and in February the family moved in. Josephine was twelve, Maria was ten, and Bion was seven. The children started school at nearby St. Hilda's and St. Hugh's Episcopal School. The apartment was close to the theaters, too, so Hugh could be home each evening for dinner. Whether he had to be at the theater early or late, everyone in the family ate together, no matter what time of the evening.

For another year and a half, Madeleine sent out *A Wrinkle in Time*. In her journal she wrote, "As for *Wrinkle*, for once I have the arrogance to know in my heart that this is something good. But if it is constantly turned down will I be able to keep the faith that I still have in it? Will I begin to doubt?"

On a cold December day in 1961, Madeleine received yet another rejection. She felt numb. More than thirty publishers had now turned down the book she loved. But because Christmas was only a week away and her mother was visiting, she tried to appear happy. She wrapped Christmas gifts, made holiday plans, and congratulated herself for handling the rejection so well. But she was performing in a numb state, and later she learned she had mixed up some of the Christmas gifts. She had given perfume to a bachelor and a necktie to a sixteen-year-old girl!

After Christmas, Madeleine told her agent, "Send

the manuscript back to me. Nobody's ever going to take it, it's too peculiar, and it just isn't fair to the family."

One evening soon after Christmas, Madeleine gave a party for her mother's friends. One of them, Hester Stover, insisted Madeleine take *A Wrinkle in Time* to her friend, John Farrar, who worked in publishing. Reluctantly, Madeleine went to see John Farrar. He said he liked her earlier books and asked what she was writing now. She handed him the manuscript of *A Wrinkle in Time*.

Two weeks later, John Farrar invited Madeleine to lunch and told her he wanted to publish *A Wrinkle in Time*. Madeleine was overjoyed! But Mr. Farrar cautioned, "Don't be disappointed if it doesn't do well. We're publishing it because we love it."

Chapter / Seven

Awards, Speeches, and Fan Mail

A Wrinkle in Time was published in 1962, and to Madeleine's surprise, it was an immediate success.

One morning in 1963, after Madeleine bustled her children off to school, the telephone rang. It was a woman named Ruth Gagliardo, from the Newbery-Caldecott committee. The Newbery Medal is the most prestigious award in children's literature. Ruth Gagliardo told Madeleine that *A Wrinkle in Time* had won the 1963 Newbery Medal.

Madeleine was shocked and surprised. She could hardly speak.

After talking briefly with Ruth, Madeleine hung up the phone, then flew through the dining room and the living room. She burst open the bedroom door, and leaped on the bed to tell Hugh the fabulous news.

She soon set to work writing a speech that she would deliver in July at the Newbery Medal acceptance ceremony. Madeleine threw away one speech after another—none of them captured what she wanted to say. Finally, she wrote a simple talk, sharing the ideas she cared about most, and left it at that.

The night of the award ceremony, Madeleine felt nervous. She was glad that Hugh could be there with her. Two hundred people—editors, publishers, librarians, and teachers—filled the beautifully decorated ballroom of Chicago's Hilton Hotel.

When it was her turn to speak, Madeleine talked about how important imagination is in a child's life. "Very few children have any problem with the world of the imagination," she said. "It's their own world, the world of their daily life, and it's our loss that so many of us grow out of it."

Soon after she finished her speech, the lights dimmed, and a white-uniformed cook pushed in a cart that held a huge cake. It was shaped like the Newbery Medal! Gold frosting lined the cake and one hundred lighted candles made it a dazzling sight.

After the ceremony, Madeleine chatted with some of the guests. One editor who had rejected *Meet the Austins* and *A Wrinkle in Time* told her, "I know I should have published these books. But I wonder: If I had accepted *A Wrinkle in Time*, would it have been

The Franklin family in 1963, the year that Madeleine won the Newbery Medal.

the right moment for it? If it had been published then, maybe you wouldn't be here now."

Madeleine knew this editor was right—the public might not have been ready for her "peculiar" book before 1963. "If *A Wrinkle in Time* had been sold right away," said Madeleine, "instead of going from publisher to publisher all that awful long time, it might have been published and just quietly died."

A Wrinkle in Time taught Madeleine a lesson about rejection and patience. But even so, she never wanted to go through years of rejection again. When her work was rejected or criticized, she felt great pain. Her books were about ideas that were important to her, and she wanted to share these thoughts with others. Madeleine knew she would always write, no matter what, but it was her deepest desire to have her work published, so she could share it with other people.

For now, though, Madeleine didn't need to worry about rejection. As the winner of the Newbery Medal, she was a celebrity and was invited to many literary parties. Often at these gatherings, a publisher would tell her, "I wish you had sent the book to us."

In every case, Madeleine answered, "But I did."

When one publisher insisted she hadn't sent *A Wrinkle in Time* to him, Madeleine showed him the journal entry in which she recorded his company's rejection.

Surprised, the publisher insisted, "But *I* never saw it. It never got to me."

He was right. Because publishing companies receive thousands of manuscripts every year, most of the stories are read by junior editors who decide which ones are good enough to be sent on to senior editors for second readings. Many of the junior editors who read *A Wrinkle in Time* rejected it, knowing that unusual books do not often sell well. This happened in many of the publishing houses to which Madeleine sent her book.

But by giving the manuscript directly to John Farrar and Hal Vursell, a senior editor at Farrar, Straus

and Cudahy, Madeleine was sure *A Wrinkle in Time*
would be given serious consideration. Like the junior
editors at other companies who had read the story
before, Mr. Vursell thought *A Wrinkle in Time* was
uncommon. But he also believed people would like it
and buy it. Like all editors, Mr. Vursell occasionally
published unique books. Sometimes they sold well,
other times they didn't. When they didn't, he felt
terrible and went back to publishing ordinary books for
a while. Luckily, Mr. Vursell received the manuscript
of *A Wrinkle in Time* when he was ready to try
something out of the ordinary again.

After the book had won the Newbery Medal, Mr.
Vursell was asked why he decided to publish *A Wrinkle
in Time* when so many other people had turned it
down. He replied, "It was our own good fortune that
the manuscript reached us at a moment when we were
ready to do battle again."

Farrar and Straus's courage made Madeleine a
literary star. Within the next two years, *A Wrinkle in
Time* won several more awards: The American Library
Association's Notable Book Award, the Lewis Carroll
Shelf Award, the Hans Christian Andersen Runner-up
Award, and the Sequoyah Award.

This success did not make Madeleine feel vain or
arrogant. But she did gain a delicious feeling of free-
dom. She no longer had to prove that she was a real

writer and she could now experiment more with her writing. Madeleine knew that experimenting was the only way she would grow as a writer, and she appreciated that Farrar and Straus encouraged her to try different kinds of writing.

It wasn't only award committees that were impressed by A Wrinkle in Time. Soon Madeleine was receiving many fan letters from children, parents, teachers, and librarians who loved A Wrinkle in Time. They all seemed to agree with one young girl who said, "I know a good book when I read it, and A Wrinkle in Time is a good book."

Madeleine felt a great responsibility to the people who read her books, saying, "Like it or not, [writers] either add to the darkness of indifference and out-and-out evil which surround us or [they] light a candle to see by." She worked harder than ever to write stories that touched people and showed them how good could conquer evil.

Most of Madeleine's fans were touched by her writing, and they wanted to meet her. She received invitations to visit schools and libraries all over the United States. She accepted some of the requests, and made friends everywhere she went. Often, these friends wrote her and Madeleine wrote back. But she was careful to limit her time spent traveling. Her job was to write, and she had children at home who needed her.

"No matter how [important] writing is to her," said Hugh, "her family always seems to come first. To the world of literature she may be a writer who happens to be a mother, but to three children she is Mother, a warm, exciting woman who happens to be a writer."

But being both a writer and a mother was not easy for Madeleine. She rose early in the mornings to get her children off to school, then stayed up late each night to see Hugh when he came home from the theater.

These long days exhausted her, and her writing and health began to suffer. One night, Madeleine finally called a family conference and told the children, "Your father needs me more in the evening when he comes home from the theater than you do in the morning before school. We don't like each other very much in the morning, anyhow. I'll get everything ready for you the night before, but you'll have to get yourselves up and dressed and off to school. When you get home in the afternoon I'm yours, all yours. But if you want a living mother this is how we'll have to manage."

One afternoon, the Franklin children came home from school begging Madeleine to make a cake for the school's bake sale. She did, but the cake turned out lopsided. Madeleine sent a note to school that said, "...Is there anything else I could do, more in line with my talents? Is there a play we could help with, or anything like that?"

Within a week, Madeleine and Hugh were directing the school's Christmas pageant. The practices took place at the Cathedral of St. John the Divine and the performance would be there also.

During the rehearsals, the young actors filled the normally quiet church with noise. One priest, Canon Edward West, was unhappy about the children interrupting the church's serene atmosphere. But Madeleine didn't care about the noise. It was more important to her that the children take part in this pageant at the church. She wanted them to understand that Christmas is not only about Santa Claus and receiving gifts—she wanted the children exposed to the meaning of Christmas.

For a time, Madeleine and the canon avoided each other because of these differences in opinion. But because the cathedral was also the Franklins' church, it was clear the two could not avoid each other forever. Finally, Madeleine tried to explain to the canon why the children's noisy presence in the church was important.

"Don't you understand," she asked the canon, "that many of them won't have any Christmas otherwise? They won't even go to church."

This conversation opened the door to the beginnings of a friendship with Canon West that grew deeper year by year, and he became a great force and inspiration in Madeleine's life.

Writing continued to be a powerful force in Madeleine's life, too. It was as essential to her as eating and breathing, yet she never seemed to have as many hours to write as she wanted. When particularly busy days or weeks kept her away from her writing for too long, she became cranky and irritable. Though Madeleine didn't always notice this herself, her family did. On one of these days, Josephine said, "Mother, you've been getting cross and edgy with us, and you haven't been doing much writing. We wish you'd get back to the typewriter."

Madeleine followed her daughter's advice. During the next three years she wrote and published three more books for children. The first, *The Moon by Night*, was another story about the Austin family. The ideas for this story came from the Franklins' 1959 cross-country camping trip, and the book was published in 1963. In 1964 came another Austin family story, called *The Twenty-Four Days Before Christmas*. *The Arm of the Starfish* was published in 1965. It was the first book in which Canon Tallis appeared, a character similar to the real-life Canon West.

By 1965, Madeleine had published a total of eleven books. Many people would be satisfied with this accomplishment and stop writing. But not Madeleine. She was just beginning!

Chapter/ Eight

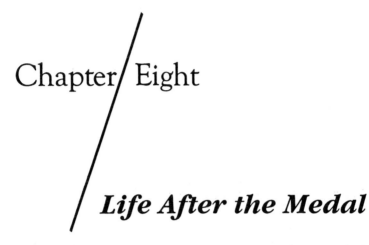

Life After the Medal

All of Madeleine's children left home during the summer of 1966—Josephine got married, Maria went off to college, and fourteen-year-old Bion left home to start boarding school.

Madeleine thought the Franklin apartment would be peaceful with her children gone. It wasn't! The telephone seemed to ring constantly and Madeleine wasn't able to write as much as she wished. One day, she wandered into the cathedral's library searching for a quiet place to write.

The library was serene, comfortable, and it contained a large collection of books. Beyond the big bay windows was a view of the beautiful cathedral courtyard.

The next morning, Madeleine gathered her paper

and felt tip markers and walked back to the cathedral library to write. She spent several quiet days in the library working on a play for the children at St. Hilda's and St. Hugh's School. But just when she was ready to type her play, the librarian announced he was leaving for jury duty. What would happen to the library? Eyeing his typewriter, Madeleine offered to watch over the library while he was gone if she could use the typewriter. The librarian accepted her offer, and Madeleine sat down at his desk to type.

Her new job gave her plenty of free time to type her play and do other writing. When days passed and Madeleine learned that the librarian had decided not to return at all, she took over his job permanently on a volunteer basis. Every morning, she filled a thermos with coffee and walked with her dogs to the cathedral. Then she wrote in the quiet library while her dogs slept under her desk or romped in the yard with the other dogs that lived on the cathedral grounds.

As always, Madeleine also continued to read a great deal. Some of her favorite books were about astrophysics, the study of physics and space. These books challenged her imagination and made her think about how new knowledge could be used to make life better for people all over the world. She also read books by theologians that helped her see how love made people grow and how hate turned people toward evil.

From both fields of study came an idea for a book about a mad scientist who tried to take over New York City. It was called *The Young Unicorns* and was published in 1968.

In 1969, Hugh was hired to play one of the leading male roles on a daytime television show called *All My Children*. Audiences loved Charles Tyler, the wealthy and sophisticated doctor that Hugh played. Wherever he went, he was recognized as Dr. Tyler and asked for his autograph. The show kept him busy, but he also continued to act in live theater, so his days and nights were both filled with his career responsibilities.

Each summer, Madeleine and Hugh moved back to Crosswicks. Their children came to visit when they could, and Madeleine's mother visited, too. By the early 1970s, Josephine and her husband had two young daughters, making the Crosswicks summers a gathering of four generations.

Though Madeleine cherished having her family around her at Crosswicks, she needed private moments every day. At times, she retreated to her quiet study to write. Other times, she took walks across the pastures to a brook where she sat and thought.

The summer of 1972 brought an end to the four-generational summers. Madeleine's ninety-year-old mother died. Madeleine felt a tremendous loss and she wrote a book about her mother's life as she grieved.

Soon after her mother's death, Madeleine was once again stricken by her childhood illness, iritis. This time, the iritis was complicated by another eye disease, glaucoma. Unfortunately, the medication for iritis made the glaucoma worse.

Madeleine continued to write in spite of her illness. A Murry family story, *A Wind in the Door*, was published during this period. Madeleine's doctor was eventually able to bring the eye diseases under control, but for a long time Madeleine feared she might go blind.

Then, for some unknown reason, Madeleine became allergic to the eye drops that were used to treat her iritis. Headaches plagued her and she could do little work. A friend who came to visit one day could tell that Madeleine felt crippling pain and asked, "If it's going to go on like this, wouldn't you rather be blind?"

"No!" Madeleine cried. She would do anything to keep her sight.

After much experimentation, Madeleine's doctor finally found a medicine that would treat Madeleine's eyes without giving her headaches. Throughout her illness, she had continued her public engagements. Everywhere she spoke, people were delighted with her zest for life, and they admired her honesty. She talked about her mistakes and failures, and about questions in life for which she had no answers.

Madeleine continued her speaking engagements in spite of her iritis and glaucoma.

People sometimes asked Madeleine why she wrote children's books. She told them she wrote for children when she had something important to say that adults wouldn't like hearing! She explained that young people are often able to understand ideas that adults can't. "Children," said Madeleine, "are excited by new ideas; they have not yet closed the doors and windows of their imagination."

One of Madeleine's frequent places to speak was Wheaton College in Wheaton, Illinois. In the mid-1970s, a Wheaton professor, Dr. Clyde Kilby, asked her if the college could make a special collection of her interviews, awards, and photographs. Madeleine agreed to his proposal, and in 1976 Wheaton College began collecting Madeleine's papers and photographs. Today, it has a large and growing amount of material about Madeleine.

In the meantime, Madeleine finished *Dragons in the Waters* and it was published in 1976. *A Swiftly Tilting Planet* was published in 1978. Together, *A Wrinkle in Time*, *A Wind in the Door*, and *A Swiftly Tilting Planet* made up what Madeleine called The Time Trilogy. Each of the books involved the Murry family and time travel. The stories were all modern-day fairy tales—part real, part fantasy, and part science fiction.

When Madeleine turned sixty-two in 1980, she was well recognized as an important writer. She had

Madeleine and Hugh in 1977, still loving and devoted to each other.

already published thirty books, including fourteen for children, and she had also won eight major awards.

Her personal life was full and satisfying, too. She and Hugh had been married for thirty-four years, and they enjoyed each other's company now more than ever. One day, Madeleine found herself discussing marriage with a taxi cab driver. She told him how long she and Hugh had been married, then wondered aloud if that might be a record for a writer and an actor.

The taxi driver whirled around in his seat and pro-
claimed, "Lady, that's not a record. That's a miracle."

Madeleine cared deeply about her marriage. She
once said the most important thing she and Hugh had
done for their children was to love each other.

She cared, too, about the quality of her writing.
Because many of her plots centered around the latest
developments in science, Madeleine was continually
reading scientific books and journals. Some of her
books, such as *A Ring of Endless Light*, required months
of research.

When Madeleine finished the research for a book,
she then spent hundreds of hours writing and revising.
When she first wrote *A House Like a Lotus*, the main
character was Vicky Austin. But the finished manuscript
didn't seem right—Vicky's personality didn't fit the
events of the story. Another of Madeleine's characters,
Poly O'Keefe, was much better suited for the part,
thought Madeleine. So she rewrote the whole book,
changing people and situations to fit her new main
character. By the time the book was published,
Madeleine had rewritten it five times. This was not
unusual. "Books," Madeleine says, "are not written.
They are rewritten."

Madeleine doesn't always know where her material
needs improvement. Quite often, she relies on others
to help her. Hugh became Madeleine's best and

harshest critic. But sometimes his suggestions frustrated her, and angrily she would take the dog for a walk while her mind worked over his criticism. When she returned, she would revise the work and then admit how much Hugh's suggestions had improved the story!

In 1985, as a result of a speech she made for an overseas radio program, Madeleine was invited to Egypt as an unofficial ambassador of goodwill for the United States Information Agency. But a few weeks before leaving, she broke her shoulder and could not go alone. Luckily, Hugh was free and able to go along. In Egypt, Madeleine and Hugh gave speeches and readings and spoke about their work.

The two were such a success that the Information Agency asked them to tour China during the spring of 1986. In China, Madeleine and Hugh made friends with Chinese people and helped them see what "real" Americans were like. Madeleine believes that one of the best things they did there was to stand on a street corner and let curious Chinese people touch them.

The trip was fulfilling for another reason. An atmosphere of total love had settled over Madeleine and Hugh. Occasionally, they went off by themselves to walk in the spring air, holding hands and enjoying the quiet time together. Even the Franklins' Chinese guide felt the power of their affection and commented, "You have a very happy marriage."

When they returned in May, Madeleine went on a lecture tour. While she was gone, Hugh saw his doctor about a minor illness and was shocked to learn he had cancer. Shortly after Madeleine returned, Hugh had to be hospitalized. He was given chemotherapy, a treatment that sometimes destroys cancer. But it did not destroy Hugh's. His cancer spread rapidly and caused other medical problems.

By the end of the summer, Hugh was too ill to leave the hospital, and it was clear he would not get well. He grew weaker with each passing day. He spent the days napping and Madeleine stayed with him the entire time. She took her portable typewriter to the hospital to work, and wrote while her husband slept.

Hugh died in September, only four months after his cancer had been discovered. Madeleine was at his side when he died, holding his body close to hers.

Madeleine was overcome by great waves of sorrow. Her children and friends came to Crosswicks to be with her, and she appreciated their loving kindness. But nothing could ease the suffering Hugh's death had caused. She was changed forever, and though she knew that grieving the loss of a loved one is healthy and important, she was in deep pain. "We are not supposed to get over our greatest griefs," she said. "They are a part of what makes us who we are."

One day, Madeleine's friend Pat came to visit.

Together, they went to see Pat's newborn grandchild. When the baby fell asleep in Madeleine's arms, Madeleine saw it as a metaphor of the rhythm of life, death, and birth. "[I am] full of memory of the forty years of Hugh's and my marriage," said Madeleine. "[The memory] helps me keep on with my work, and that is what Hugh would want me to do." Not long afterward she began work on a book about her marriage to Hugh.

Chapter/Nine

Stars to Lighten the Darkness

Today, Madeleine still lives in her New York City apartment for part of the year. Her two eldest grandchildren, Charlotte and Lena, live with her. She often teaches a writing class at St. Hilda's and St. Hugh's and works at the cathedral, where she is called a writer-in-residence. She also continues to write in her journal, as she has for almost all of her life.

Madeleine receives about one hundred fan letters each week. Approximately one-quarter of them are from young people. Children tell her they have read all of her books and many say they have read them over and over again.

In some letters, children ask Madeleine how they can become writers. She advises them to keep a journal about their thoughts and feelings. Madeleine's old

Madeleine playing the piano, one of her favorite pastimes. She believes a writer must practice writing daily, just as a professional piano player must practice his or her instrument every day.

journals are a constant source of information for her as she writes stories. When she needs to know how a thirteen year old might feel about an experience, she studies the journal that she wrote when she was thirteen.

Madeleine says journal writing is good for another reason. Just as a piano player must practice at the piano each day, writers must practice writing daily. A journal is a good way to accomplish this.

But Madeleine cautions that writing is hard work. Great ideas do not always come before writing, she points out, and real writers do not wait to write until they have the perfect idea. First, they sit down and write, and many times the writing itself inspires creative ideas.

"The hardest part of writing a book," says Madeleine, "is making yourself sit down at the typewriter and bat out a first page, any kind of a first page, knowing that it will be changed over and over again before the book is done. But there will never be a book without this rough beginning."

Children also ask Madeleine where she gets her ideas for stories. She explains, "Everything I do, everywhere I go, everybody I meet—I see story. Story springs from experience, and then the storyteller goes on. When I actually start to write, I listen to the characters; I listen to the story; and almost always new ideas come flooding in as I write."

Madeleine says she keeps various stories in her imagination like pots of food warming on the back of the stove. As a new idea comes along, she drops it into the right pot. Then when a book is finished, she starts another, dipping into the pot that is shouting the loudest to be written.

Madeleine reminds these aspiring writers that writing is hard work.

Adults write letters to Madeleine, too. Some write to say they enjoyed her books written for grown-ups; others write to tell her how much they like her children's books. Madeleine knows her children's books are enjoyed by people of all ages. But she is quick to point out that writing children's books is no easier than writing books for adults. "If it's not good enough for adults, it's not good enough for children," she insists. As she writes, Madeleine never thinks about the age of

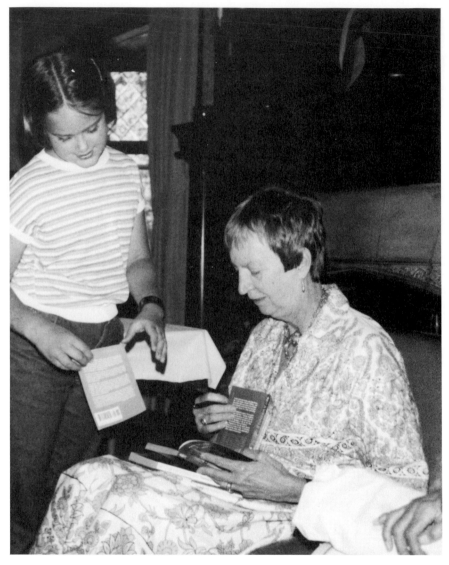

Madeleine autographs some of her novels for a young fan.

her audience or whether or not people will like her book. Instead, she concentrates on telling the best story possible.

Once or twice a month, she travels to a church, library, or university, where she teaches, delivers a speech, or autographs books. She has been invited to almost every state in the United States and to many countries around the world. But Madeleine tries not to travel too much, knowing that her main job is to stay home and write.

Now Bion lives at Crosswicks year-round with his wife, and Madeleine loves to visit them, especially at Christmastime. Occasionally, Josephine, her husband, and their youngest child also come to visit Madeleine and the girls from their home in San Francisco. Maria and her husband visit when they can, too. They live in nearby Essex, Connecticut, with their two young sons. As often as possible, Madeleine and her grandchildren carry on a family tradition of birthday parties in the apple orchard at Crosswicks, with presents and balloons tied to the "birthday trees."

When Madeleine turned seventy in 1988, her granddaughter gave a birthday party for her. Three hundred people came from all over the world to honor Madeleine at a spectacular affair at the cathedral. It was a night she would never forget.

Today, Madeleine is in constant demand. Being

Crosswicks at Christmastime.

both a popular children's author and a popular author of adult books has resulted in hundreds of thousands of fans. Though she vows monthly to cut back her speaking and touring engagements, the next request always seems "too good to pass up." To date, Madeleine has published twenty books for children, and she shows little sign of slowing down. She will continue to write as long as she has a story to tell.

Madeleine believes a good book can be "explosive material, a living star to lighten the darkness." In remaining devoted to her lifelong dream to be a writer, Madeleine has created many stars that have lightened the hearts of millions of readers. And her stars will endure, to brighten the lives of generations to come.

Selected Bibliography

Franklin, Hugh. "Madeleine L'Engle." *Horn Book.* (August 1963): 356–360.

L'Engle, Madeleine. *A Circle of Quiet.* San Francisco: Harper and Row, 1972.

——. "The Expanding Universe." *Horn Book.* (August 1963): 351–355.

——. *The Irrational Season.* San Francisco: Harper and Row, 1977.

——. "Nomaste!" *Ashley Hall Newsletter.* July 1, 1982. 1–10.

——. "Regina Medal Recipient–Madeleine L'Engle." *Catholic Library World.* July–August 1984. 28–31.

——. *The Summer of the Great-Grandmother.* San Francisco: Harper and Row, 1974.

——. *Two-Part Invention: The Story of a Marriage.* New York: Farrar, Straus, and Giroux, 1988.

Index